PARIS

Sidewalk café

Paris

by IRENE SMITH

Illustrated by EMIL WEISS

 RAND McNALLY & COMPANY

CHICAGO   NEW YORK   SAN FRANCISCO

Dedicated to
Simon and Dorothea Lissim
with a great debt of gratitude

CONTENTS

ILLUSTRATIONS

7

PARIS

I.

HOME OF THE PARISIANS

Where the River Seine bends toward the sea, in the midlands of northern France, stands the great capital, Paris, city of art and of pleasure. She has been called the Queen of Cities, the City of Light, and Gay Paree. When it is time to go on a journey, no travelers are happier than those who are bound for Paris. They will find that she is very old, yet supremely modern, and beautiful—many say the most beautiful city in the world. Artists and students from everywhere, and tourists in throngs, are drawn by their hopes and dreams to Paris.

The main roads of Europe lead to Paris from the east and southwest, over mountains and plains, and across France's fertile provinces. Atlantic Ocean liners dock at the ports of Cherbourg and Le Havre, where trains stand ready for the fast trip inland to Paris. The rails throb as the trains cross Normandy's meadows, into the valley of the Seine River, leaving cathedral towns and factories, passing hedgerows, orchards, and truck farms. They run through the city suburbs and come to a halt in Gare St.-Lazare, their station in Paris.

Planes from Africa, from England, from all directions, glide in over two markers familiar to the world: a curving river and a slim, sheer tower—the Seine River and the Eiffel Tower. In the misty light they head for a landing on the outskirts, at Orly or Bourget. This is Paris, with excitement in the air and traffic in confusion. Voices are French, words pour in torrents, and spirits start rising.

Here the citizens of Paris do their work and spend their leisure in the ways that are their own. Other people feel the freedom of the place and make themselves at home in its atmosphere. Eager to know the city, sightseers stream through art galleries and museum palaces, churches, shops, and restaurants, absorbed by the wonders that the French have created.

At sidewalk cafés Parisians drink their morning coffee, basking in the sun. These outdoor restaurants are not merely popular in Paris, they are her normal habit. The wide clean pavements allow generous space for customers, and are shaded in summer by trees and awnings. When the warm air of May brings tables and chairs outdoors, the long season of mild weather has begun. Even late in autumn, when chestnut trees drop their green and yellow leaves, open air places still are comfortable and attract their crowds.

There are cafés to suit every taste and every member of the family. While Papa enjoys his glass of wine, the waiter pours soft drinks or milk for the children. On every street the large and small cafés spread out across the sidewalks on fair days, and shrink close to the buildings when it rains. All day long their patrons come and go, taking time to sit for a while with food and drink, to watch the rest of the world go by.

Street crowds stroll on the wide avenues and boulevards that stretch away in many directions. The sun seems to shine through a glistening haze and the whole scenery sparkles under a pearly sky. Pedestrians take their time, but automobiles and motorbikes rush and tangle in a headlong hurry. Buses and taxis roll past sculptured fountains, across little squares, through bustling streets that are crowded and old, and along avenues with stately lawns and flowerbeds. Traffic thunders across the bridges. Visitors look for a tall steel spire against the sky, and recognize the Eiffel Tower, the emblem of Paris. In the opposite direction they catch occasional glimpses of another well-known landmark, the great white dome of the Church of Sacré-Coeur. The street most of them want to find first of all is the Champs-Elysées, known the world over for its handsome appearance and luxury trade.

The Seine River, *la Seine* to all Parisians, flows for eight miles through the city and under its thirty-three bridges. It divides Paris into North and South, or Right and Left. The North Side is called the Right Bank, and all that lies south of the river is the famous Left Bank. An island between these banks, the Ile de la Cité, has an important place in the life story of the city. Notre Dame Cathedral, standing on this island in the river, is one of the spectacles that give meaning to Paris.

Carved stone walls, mellowed by time and weather, are the special beauty of Paris buildings. But the modern age demands to be admitted, and changes are coming in.

A typical Parisian street—

A house hundreds of years old, with its ornate arches and wrought-iron scrolls, gives way to bold new steel and glass. Today's effects have not yet sharpened the face of Paris, but motors overcrowd the streets. When progress presses for its rights, the old city seems to tolerate it.

The industrial twentieth century necessarily brings big factory methods and modern machinery. These make it harder for the family trades to earn a living. Parisians much prefer to run their own concerns, however small. One-room factories, repair works, and craft trades of many

shops below, apartments above

kinds struggle for a living on a modest scale. These little industries can be seen on every street, undoubtedly in the same spot for a hundred years, with the owners' apartments above them.

France has been called a nation of shopkeepers. Small retail stores, bordering ordinary streets and squares, are family affairs handed down from father to son. So many people live with or near their businesses that a street of homes may look half commercial. Even the finer residential sections have a few shops and a café or two.

No one living in Paris need go far for his ordinary wants. The bakery shop is on the corner, giving out its fragrant smell of *croissants* and *brioches* hot from the oven, between four and five o'clock in the morning. Parisians are enormous consumers of bread, and who would blame them, considering the crusty goodness of long French loaves? Children carrying some home from the bakery, unwrapped, in the French manner, possibly nibble a bite or two as they trudge along. The neighborhood stores in every block include small fruit and vegetable markets, the *charcuterie*, where cold meats, salads, and canned foods are sold, and a pharmacy. The ever-present *Tabac* signs hang over cafés, to show where tobacco may be bought, although the government controls its sale. A barber shop is nearby, and a stationery store supplies newspapers, which are printed morning and evening in the rue Montmartre.

Parish churches and public schools are of course the prominent buildings in home communities. Schools are usually large enough to include all the divisions—the kindergarten and infant schools, the primary, and then high primary schools. Students next attend the *lycée*, or else a technical school. French *lycées* correspond to high schools in the United States, but they include advanced studies amounting to about one year of college work.

Paris streets are famous for their confusing habit of changing names every few blocks. A great many of them honor well-known men and women and at least two hundred pay homage to saints. There are four thousand streets in Paris, or six hundred miles of them, some bearing the titles of such unforgettable Frenchmen as Lafayette, Riche-

Inside the subway (Metro)

lieu, Haussmann, Voltaire, Hugo, and Zola. Leaders of other countries too have streets as memorials. Five Americans chosen for this distinction are George Washington, Benjamin Franklin, Woodrow Wilson, General Pershing, and Franklin D. Roosevelt. The English language has benefitted by adopting from the French two handy nouns, *avenue* and *boulevard*.

Bicycles still mingle with heavier traffic on busy thoroughfares, as thousands ride to work. Few Parisians need to travel long distances each day, because they manage to live in a convenient area. The subway system (their *Metro*) is therefore relieved of rush hour crowds and top-speed schedules. Subway trains are comfortable and clean and their two networks connect every corner of the city.

Parisians are hard-working people. They open their businesses early, run them efficiently, and produce much. However, they are loyal to customary ways, and like their two free hours at midday. They are thrifty with money, but able and happy to spend time. Leisure is popular and its uses are pleasant, including sitting at sidewalk cafés or promenading on the Boulevards near the Opera. Here where traffic is heaviest, sidewalks widest, and outdoor tables thickest, is the Parisians' personal domain, their own favorite section of Paris that has everything they love most.

Benches to comfort weary walkers,

Strolling up and down the Champs-Elysées and along the banks of the Seine River the people continually absorb the beauty and interest of their city. It is always easy to find a place to sit and rest, for there are the many cafés, as well as benches placed under the trees, to comfort weary walkers. Paris is full of trees, especially plane trees and the much-prized horsechestnuts. They spread their shade along the pavements and across the old cobblestones, as though the well-worn streets of Paris were renewed by their green life, and meant to last forever.

The city's twenty thousand acres are divided into

shaded by horsechestnut trees

A Paris policeman (gendarme)

twenty municipal districts, which the French call *arron-dissements*. Fourteen are on the Right Bank, six on the Left, and each has its mayor. The city as a whole is governed by a Municipal Council and a chief administrator called the Prefect of the Seine Department. The police are easy-going and polite, but well armed. Their becoming caps and swinging capes lend style and a touch of gallantry to the Paris scene. The fame of the French *gendarmes* has spread beyond their native land.

Parks encircle Paris, and squares and public gardens dot her interior, totaling six hundred acres of open space within the city and thousands more just outside. Parisians are park enthusiasts, so they make full use of their chances for outdoor recreation. It is their custom to pay a small fee, twenty *centimes*, for occupying a public garden chair. The elegant Avenue Foch leads west to an important park, the famous Bois de Boulogne, which covers twenty-one hundred forested acres. Its lakes and islands, cascades and fountains provide some enchanting scenery. The Bois de Vincennes is another very large park outside the city limits, home of the Paris zoo. Scarcely noticeable moats and barriers allow wild animals to roam freely, without need of cages. Rocky ledges and protected vales make natural settings similar to those of the animals' origins. Vincennes and Boulogne were once royal hunting parks.

Wild animals roam freely in the Paris Zoo

Admirers of plant life find their special pleasure in the Jardin des Plantes (Garden of Plants), which lies along the Left Bank east of the midtown section. It is the botanical garden of Paris, to be counted among the beauty spots. Two other parks that serve Paris with distinction are the Parc Monceau and Parc de Montsouris.

Paris, the capital of France, lies ninety miles from the sea, in a basin surrounded by hills. The hills—Saint Cloud, Sèvres, Mont Valerian, among them—are blamed for the frequent mist and rain, but the weather is never extremely warm or cold. A century and a half ago when Napoleon was emperor, seven hundred thousand Parisians made up the metropolis. It has since grown to five million, making Paris second only to London, which is the largest European city.

Continually growing outward, metropolitan Paris has a suburban population now greater than that within the city proper. The major financial, civil, commercial, and industrial strength of France is concentrated in and near Paris, and provides livelihood for the city's millions. The heavy iron and steel industries, and the chemical and engineering firms have moved to suburban towns that cluster on the rim of Paris, such as Boulogne-Billancourt and Sèvres, while atomic energy plants are in Saclay.

Beyond these busy suburbs the countryside around Paris is known historically as the Ile de France. It is green, wooded, and ornamented with residences built as palaces for former kings and nobility. Best known of these is Versailles, once the grand estate of Louis XIV. The elaborate palace is surrounded by formal gardens which are

Versailles

a national show place, with their lovely lakes and endless
fountains. Fontainebleau, the best-loved palace of Napoleon, had housed monarchs from the sixteenth century.
It still stands among glades and streams in a vast preserve.
Napoleon saw its charms for the last time on an April day
in 1814, when, defeated and deposed, he bade his personal
troops farewell.

The roads that wind through the Ile de France soon
turn back toward Paris. Some of the reasons for the appeal of the city may be argued, but everyone agrees on one
of them. That one is her restaurants. Dining in Paris is an
experience usually described in terms of rapture. It has

Fontainebleau

inspired poets and philosophers. Men and women in the far-off corners of earth make themselves happy just talking about it.

French cooking formed one of the earliest bonds of international understanding, and the bond remains. Paris possesses the most treasured secrets of this skill, for the country's expert chefs are claimed, naturally, by hotels and restaurants in the capital. Fine cooking is considered an art, and a successful cook commands very high respect.

Of course there are restaurants of every kind and size in every great city. Paris has her full share of those which are world famous, and very expensive, where choicest foods and wines are served in surroundings of luxury. But the typical Paris restaurant is a modest place, where only the food is important. It may be large and prominently located, or part of a plain house on a side street. Its rooms are full of the smells of cheeses, herbs, and wine.

Most sidewalk cafés have indoor space and at meal-time nearly all cafés become restaurants. Customers usually go inside for dinner, unless the place is very small or the day uncomfortably warm. A family may be the proprietors of a typical neighborhood restaurant, with a few tables set in the front room, and living quarters in the rear. The dinner is cooked to order, so while Monsieur enthuses about the specialties being prepared, the hungry guests live for an hour on fragrances from the kitchen. There Madame is broiling mushrooms and spooning her seasonings over entrées that promise perfection. In even the humblest places crusty bread and a bottle of red wine are on the table.

French cooks create sauces for meats and fish that give them distinguished flavor and aroma. Their delicate soufflés and their soups and pastries long ago set a standard for all civilized countries.

From architecture to omelettes, from monuments to millinery, the choicest and most important of everything French is found in Paris. The country's machinery of government, her historic treasures, and most of her material resources are kept within the capital. Beyond the city lie the provinces, which send her supplies. They do not challenge the right of Paris, as one of the world's cultural centers, to own the art and history of France.

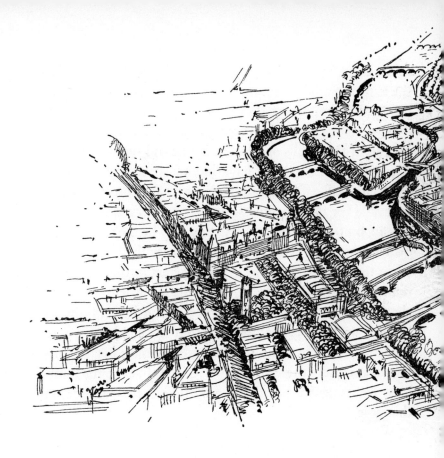

THE ISLANDS AND THE RIVER

The oldest and most important thoroughfare in Paris is not, as might be thought, the Champs-Elysées, but the Seine River. It flows in a broad curve through the heart of the city and plays a tremendous part in its life. Paris is necessarily a river port, depending upon floating barges

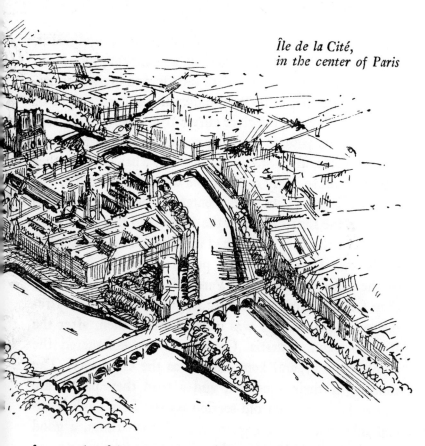

*Île de la Cité,
in the center of Paris*

for much of its commerce. They bring in food supplies and haul away merchandise by the millions of tons. The Seine is a picturesque river. Writers far back in the Middle Ages often mentioned its beauty. Old prints show that through the centuries trade has made full demands on the deep Seine channel. But sometimes, on a smoky morning, it looks like a mere canal.

The Seine is a pleasure stream to the Parisians who walk on its banks and bridges, and to the men and boys enjoying their fishing. There is always something to be seen along its course. Strong embankments have tamed it, yet the Seine has a will of its own, and varying moods. In summer the river does its work quietly and invites leisure, but in winter it can be very difficult. Taking its right of way through Paris, the river curves from east to west, separating in its passage to make room for two islands, the Ile de la Cité and Ile St.-Louis, joined by a bridge. No other city has built so many roads across water for its traffic.

The Ile de la Cité in the center of Paris is a crossroads between the Left Bank and the Right. On this vital, busy "Island of the City" Paris had its origin. The first settlers in the dim long ago were a peaceful band of fishermen of the Celtic tribes, called Parisii. Surrounded by water, they felt safe from unfriendly neighbors, and so they remained. Their village was called Lutèce; then, after the Romans came, Lutetia. Caesar's legions conquered the whole country and kept Lutetia as the chief city. The remains of their aqueduct, and a road they paved, are still to be seen in an old section on the Left Bank. Paris had sidewalks and a big arena in Roman times, a good water supply, and even parks.

During the third century, Saint Denis brought the Christian faith to Gaul, the name by which France was then known. At about that time Lutetia began to be called Paris. Later the Franks invaded Gaul and gave the country their name. When the savage Huns overran Gaul in 451, Parisians believed that Sainte Geneviève gave them her protection, and they were saved. In gratitude, they made her their patron saint.

Geneviève in her youth had tended sheep. A thousand

Gilded statue of Joan of Arc in the Place des Pyramides

years later in French history another shepherdess tried to save Paris. She was Joan of Arc. France and England were at war in the fifteenth century when Joan came from Domremy, in the province of Lorraine, to lead her king's soldiers. Paris itself had fallen to the British in 1421. Joan was nineteen when she died for France, and became the country's most beloved saint and heroine. A gilded statue of Joan on her horse stands in the Place des Pyramides. It is decorated each year on the anniversary of her death.

Close to the river and the islands the past seems less remote. Passengers on motor launches, that travel up and down the Seine, get splendid views of Paris. Imagine tak-

ing a daytime trip on one of these sightseeing boats, which
are called *bateaux mouches*. They leave regularly from a
landing near the Solferino Bridge. Nearby are the powerful walls of Notre Dame, the Roman Catholic cathedral
of Paris, rising from their ancient setting on the Ile de la
Cité. The great church looms in Gothic dignity above
its island base and gleams on the river in a broad reflection.
The launch moves away from its dock toward the Pont
Royal, or Royal Bridge. Notre Dame can be seen in its
full proportions on the return upstream.

Ivy climbs on the embankment walls. Along the street
above the pier, stone parapets and roomy pavements line
the Seine banks, where trees half hide a picturesque row
of houses. These streets that follow the river are called

the quays (*quais*) and they are rich with the flavor of Paris. Quays change their names from bridge to bridge. Below them, close to water level, are the landings for river barges, and piers for loading and unloading goods.

Soon the launch will encircle the Ile de la Cité. This island is shaped like a boat with its prow headed downstream toward the sea, moored to the banks by bridges. Its forward tip is a small green park, the Square du Vert Galant. Children play in the swings while their mothers watch, and passengers wave from the *bateau mouche*. Long barges loaded with grain from rural France drift by on the yellow-brown water. Anglers are out in small boats, and other fishermen lean from the walls to drop their lines. The river's slick surface reflects the brightness of sun

Stone bridge over Seine, bateau mouche

piercing through haze, and mirrors the arch of a stone
bridge breaking in strange colors as the ripples scatter it.
Now the well-groomed shore of Ile St.-Louis glides past
the deck. Along its serene quays the once fashionable residences still uphold their dignity. The trip continues its
island circle back to the Pont Neuf, or New Bridge.

This bridge (*pont*) was new in 1603 when Henry IV
proved it was safe by being the first to ride across it. After
the Romans, the first sidewalks to be built in Paris were
on the Pont Neuf. King Henry on his horse still rides on
the bridge. From the Pont Neuf his statue surveys modern
traffic. King Henry would have been amazed at its unend-
ing stream. The New Bridge is the oldest surviving bridge

and anglers out in small boats

in Paris still in active use, for its original foundations support the structure to this day.

From here the boat continues down the river toward several well-known bridges lying ahead. Many stories with sinister plots have been written about the Paris bridges that span the Seine. The dark night, the water lapping at the walls, the lonely figures, the stairway down to the boat landing, the *gendarmes* in their jaunty capes—these make an atmosphere of mystery and adventure.

Many of these bridges that have played so large a part in Paris life and in French fiction were built in the seventeenth century. Most of them, old and new, have been rebuilt, some of them many times. Nearly all are supported

Pont Alexander III connects

on stone arches, and nearly all are of shapely design. The regular traffic of Paris uses the bridges heavily, but three are reserved for people on foot. The favorite bridge of strollers is the romantic Pont des Arts. The Pont Alexander III is the most recent bridge, completed in 1900, and probably the most artistic, with its sculptured garlands of sea life.

Two very handsome sections of Paris that face each other across the river are connected by the Pont Alexander III. The Grand Palais and Petit Palais, on the Right Bank, have their setting in formal gardens which extend to the Champs-Elysées. On the Left Bank the span leads into the Quai d'Orsay, one of the finest streets, in an area of man-

two handsome sections of Paris

Hôtel des Invalides with park-like esplanade in front

sions and wall-enclosed gardens. Adjoining the Quai
d'Orsay a park-like esplanade forms the background for
a monumental structure, the Hôtel des Invalides. It is a
magnificent building with an outstandingly beautiful
façade.

Louis XIV issued an edict in 1670 that resulted in Les
Invalides, a place to provide better care for the soldiers
wounded in his wars. Its ten miles of corridors and rooms

for thousands of patients are almost empty of war invalids nowadays. The space is used by military museums and schools. Visitors go to Les Invalides to see Napoleon's tomb, placed with due pomp underneath the great dome in 1840. A walk was built above the tomb, encircling it, so that all who gazed on mighty Napoleon had to bow their heads.

Just past the Esplanade des Invalides it is time to watch for the unique feature of the next bridge. This Pont de l'Alma was begun in 1854, to commemorate the victory of French and English forces over the Russians at the Alma River in the Crimean War. The stone figures of four French soldiers—a grenadier, a *chasseur*, an artilleryman, and a Zouave—in the distinctive uniforms of their regiments, were erected on the center piers of the triple-arched bridge.

The Zouave soldier-statue continues to serve his countrymen by measuring the height of the Seine water level. During damp cold winters the river rises and sometimes floods Left Bank cellars. At any threat of high water, Parisians start watching the Zouave. When the water is up to his belt they call it ugly weather, and when they say, "It comes to his neck and may drown him," the river is near flood tide.

Everybody recognizes the Eiffel Tower, the popular symbol of Paris. It is so tall that it is visible from many points in the city. This ride on the river, however, brings it into full view, for as the boat rounds a curve, there it stands, from ground to dizzy pinnacle. This *Tour Eiffel* of the Parisians is a network of open girders laced together

One of the four stone soldiers under the Pont de l'Alma

and tapering upward. Two and a half million rivets join all those thousands of steel pieces, as if the tower were made with a gigantic toy construction set.

A. G. Eiffel, a steel-age pioneer, was the designer. He presented his finished wonder at the 1889 Paris Exposition, and for several years the Eiffel Tower was the tallest structure in the world. The Empire State Building in New York surpasses it by not many feet. Today it serves as a station for weather, radio, and television relay.

The elevators are busy every day taking sightseers to the tower top. There they behold a valley brimming with roofs and chimney pots stretching far away in every direction. All of Paris can be seen and, on clear days, the view extends sixty miles beyond the city. Church spires and steeples break the low skyline, but in all Paris only the airy shaft of the Eiffel Tower thrusts far above rooftop level.

On the opposite bank stands the Palais de Chaillot, a new wide-winged palace, facing the Eiffel Tower from a prominent elevation. It houses the notable Musée de l'Homme, or Museum of Man, which traces in its exhibits the history of every race. The exhibits continue to grow as explorers and scientists add new data. Other museums adjoin the palace, among them the particularly imposing Museum of Modern Art. The United Nations holds its Paris sessions below Chaillot, in modern buildings bordered by gardens and the river's edge.

Now the city's spectacles are behind and the boat approaches the Pont de Grenelle, the turning-back point. A small copy of the Statue of Liberty, the great gift to

The Eiffel Tower

America from the people of France, stands on this bridge.

Returning up the Seine, Notre Dame comes again into view, with the afternoon sun on her main façade, which faces the west. Now there is time to see the old cathedral whole against the sky, and to reflect upon the long lifetime that she has known. This builders' masterpiece in delicately carved stone is one of the most beautiful and perfect examples of Gothic design. Notre Dame is steeped in history, but even before men could record their deeds, the Parisii's pagan altars stood on her ground.

Later the Romans built a temple to Jove on the site, which in the fourth century was replaced by a Christian church. The city continued to grow and in time required a large structure for the church of the Bishops of Paris. In 1163 the cornerstone was laid for Notre Dame Cathedral. Sculptors however were still at work in 1225, hewing Biblical scenes out of the soft limestone. Generations worshipped in the unfinished cathedral until 1345, when labor finally ended.

Limestone for Notre Dame and for other construction in Paris had been found along the Seine River banks. This was a cream-colored material that cut easily and hardened gradually, after it was exposed to air. The pale rich tones of the young cathedral were of course soiled as centuries passed, and Notre Dame has long been gray with age.

Three lofty stories, topped by two towers, were the feat of master masons, who had to hoist each stone into place without the aid of machinery. Those high twin towers look across the Paris basin toward an outer rim of low hills. Victor Hugo, the great French novelist, de-

Main façade of Notre Dame Cathedral

Gargoyles on bell tower of Notre Dame

scribed the view from the North Tower as a "dazzling sea of roofs, chimneys, streets, bridges, squares, spires, and steeples."

Sculptures of saints and kings in procession ornament the massive walls. The carved portals and great stained glass windows are considered outstanding works of art. Ever since Hugo's *The Hunchback of Notre Dame* was published, in 1831, the cathedral's gargoyles have been objects of particular curiosity. They are ugly stone demons, also called grotesques, carved around the bell tower. Their cruelly cunning faces leer down over Paris as they did in the Middle Ages, when it was thought necessary to portray evil as well as good in church art. Victor Hugo's hunchback, Quasimodo, was bell-ringer for the cathedral. He lived in the tower like a human gargoyle, with these unearthly dragons, dogs, and griffins for companions.

Here at Notre Dame, Saint Louis, for whom the Ile St.-Louis is named, received his staff from the bishop and started on his first Crusade. The same aged stones have witnessed strife and bloodshed, and victories for both the righteous and the ungodly. The cathedral knew one of its most extravagant occasions in 1804, when Napoleon and Josephine were crowned rulers of France.

The Ile de la Cité is again close by as the trip on the river nears its finish. Part of the island is occupied by the Palace of Justice, along with police and fire departments and several hospitals. The big flower market near the

Night scene on the Seine River

cathedral is a main attraction. Many like to wander from it to the outdoor bookstalls that stand in Notre Dame's shadow, alongside the river.

On a clear night, when you are out for a walk, pause on a bridge, perhaps the Pont Notre Dame, for one of the most thrilling views in all Paris, taking in the islands and the river. The old cathedral is radiantly floodlit, and near it the luminous spire of Ste.-Chapelle, a small and lovely church on the Ile de la Cité, points above the rooftops. Lamps on other bridges up and down the Seine shine upon the water like strings of jewels.

III.

THE RIGHT BANK

Such well-known Paris landmarks as Champs-Elysées, Place de la Concorde, Etoile, the Louvre, the Opera, Place Vendôme, Sacré-Coeur and Montmartre, are all located in the part of the city that lies north of the Seine River. The places that bear these names give Paris much of the luster of her fine promenades, her place in art and fashion, her luxury hotels, shops, and many of her palatial residences. The Right Bank therefore can claim much of the elegance of Paris, although by no means all of it. There are rich and poor sections on both banks, and of course vast middle-class areas, as in all cities.

All parts of Paris are crossed, circled, and linked by boulevards, but when a Parisian speaks of "the Boulevards" he means a certain few. These are known as the *Grands Boulevards*, and they run in a continuous line that carves a wide semicircle through the central business region of the Right Bank. With the Church de la Madeleine at one end and the Bastille Square at the other, the Boulevards change names ten times in their course. They follow the

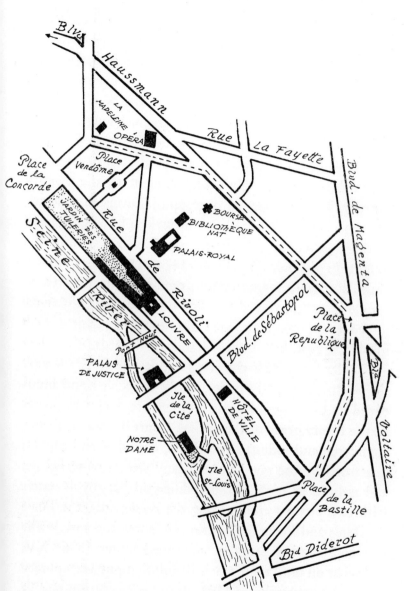

Les Grands Boulevards, following the position of the city's old ramparts

position of the city's old ramparts, which fortified its northern boundaries from the 14th to the 17th century.

By the year 1000 the French capital was becoming a city. Five times it had been occupied by enemy forces. It had outlived many weak kings, and the Norman siege, after the death of Charlemagne. Paris had long ago outgrown its original boundaries on the Ile de la Cité and was spreading far beyond both borders of the Seine. Philip Augustus brought enlightenment to the twelfth century. He got together a group of European scholars, and this group grew into the University of Paris, founded in the next century. Paris remained medieval until the long reign of Louis XIV, from 1647 to 1715. His minister, Jean-Baptiste Colbert, whose grand-scale dream was to restyle Paris, convinced the king that the walls no longer served a purpose. They were torn down and their ditches filled in, as road-bed for the Grands Boulevards.

Under Louis XIV the first great designs for Paris took shape. Buildings and squares, nobly conceived and influenced by Greek and Roman architecture, began to promise the future grace of the capital. Court life was brilliant, commerce and industry prospered, churches and schools benefitted by the good times. Many streets were lighted and policed at night. Colbert honored his royal master with two victory arches along the Boulevards, the Porte St.-Denis and Porte St.-Martin. (A *porte* is a gate.) The vast construction program continued under Louis XV, and went on until the French Revolution put a temporary end to the monarchy in 1792.

Louis XIV desired his capital to possess all possible

beauty. He ordered the creation of the Champs-Elysées, a long straight sweep of avenue through the finest part of the city. It extends from the Place de la Concorde westward to the Etoile, divided midway by a landscaped circle called the Rond Point. The Champs-Elysées east of the Rond Point gratified the king's pride in display, with palaces and grounds of spacious grandeur. It became both a park and a boulevard. The western end, not so wide, is lined with chestnut trees and ribbons of shaded lawn rolling down its entire length. These separate the traffic lanes from broad sidewalks which lure the strollers with fancy awnings, shops, and cafés. Paris is the recognized center of the world for beautiful clothes and wonderful food. The Champs-Elysées is a showplace of glitter and gaiety. It brings together people from everywhere, who have come to see and be seen, and to dine and shop. Louis XV gave the street its name. Champs-Elysées means Elysian Fields, which in mythology is Paradise.

The Place de la Concorde, where this famous street begins, is the largest square in Paris. It gives outstanding proof of the city architects' respect for space and design. The landscaping makes a setting for pavilions and statuary, and foreground for the palaces within view of the Place de la Concorde. On its eight sides huge female sculptures represent the eight French cities of Marseille, Lyon, Strasbourg, Lille, Rouen, Brest, Nantes, and Bordeaux. After the Franco-Prussian War ended in 1871, Paris students used to come every year to lay a wreath on the Strasbourg monument. This was an expression of sorrow because this chief city of Alsace-Lorraine had been ceded to Germany.

The granite column at the center of the Place de la Concorde is an ancient Egyptian obelisk, sometimes called Cleopatra's Needle, like the one in New York's Central Park. It was a Pharaoh's memorial, thirteen centuries before Christ, and a gift to France from an Egyptian viceroy in 1836. Countless objects of art in Paris are very old, but this once-pink, most aged Obelisk of Luxor occupies a place of honor. Urn-shaped fountains on each side of the obelisk form the Concorde's grand centerpiece. They are examples of the city's wealth in sculpture.

The Champs-Elysées, showing the Arc de Triomphe and a sidewalk café

The area of the square was just a neglected space in the time of Louis XIV. Its broad octagon began to take shape in 1757, the work of Jacques Gabriel, who was called the greatest eighteenth-century architect. He named it the Place Louis XV, for his king, and so it remained for about thirty-five years, until the French Revolution altered many titles.

Where automobiles now speed around the square, royal carriages once scattered commoners. But royalty's day of doom was to come, and come it did, on the four-

teenth of July in 1789, when the Bastille was stormed by Paris mobs and its walls torn down. This was the fearful old prison where the kings had kept their enemies, and its destruction started the blazing fires of revolution. At that time the main ornament in the square was a statue of the king. This the citizens wrathfully removed and melted down, to make cannon. Place de la Révolution the square then became, and it was here in 1793 that the guillotined head of Louis XVI was held aloft by the executioner. More than a thousand other Frenchmen died on the same spot before all the terror ended. Afterward the area was again renamed, becoming the Place de la Concorde, Square

Place de la Concorde, showing
urn-shaped fountain and obelisk

of Peace, to help people forget the awful things that had happened there.

The Place de la Concorde is considered the capital's second most important area, after the Etoile. On its rim stands the Elysée Palace, where the President of France lives, as well as the Bourbon Palace, home of the National Assembly, and other fine buildings including the United States Embassy. With its open plazas the Place de la Concorde is a natural place for public gatherings. One memorable May night in 1927, crowds waited hours here for news of Lindbergh's flight across the Atlantic. Every July Fourteenth, Parisians by the thousands come to celebrate Bastille Day, with flags, fireworks, and music. Like the American Fourth of July, Bastille Day stands for freedom won. Times of crisis, as well as national holidays, draw Parisians to the Place de la Concorde. Here, during World War II, men and women of the city wept as foreign soldiers marched in to occupy Paris.

From the west side of the square the Champs-Elysées climbs gently toward one of the city's commanding objects, that marks the end of the avenue. It is the largest and best-known stone arch in the world, the Arc de Triomphe, or Arch of Triumph, at the Etoile.

Napoleon began the arch in 1806 to celebrate his victories, but a few years later he fell from power. Finally in 1836 the Arc de Triomphe was finished under Louis-Philippe, the Citizen King, and dedicated "To all French armies since 1792." At its feet lie reminders of two world wars in the twentieth century, the tomb of France's Unknown Soldier, and the Eternal Light, a flame that burns

TOP: *Elysée Palace;* CENTER: *United States Embassy;* BOTTOM: *Bourbon Palace*

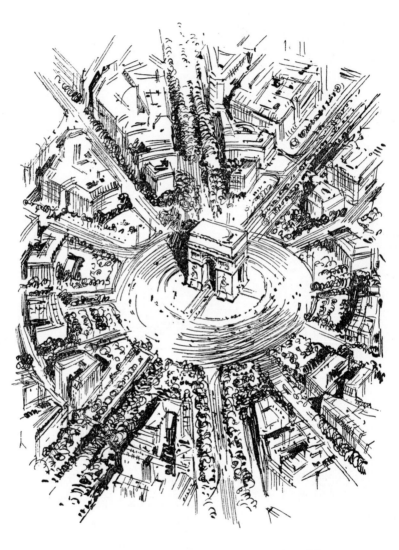

Arc de Triomphe, in center of Place de l'Etoile, with avenues forming twelve spokes around it

in memory of those who died defending France. The Unknown Soldier was chosen from the unidentified among France's war dead, just as the Unknown Soldier buried in Arlington Cemetery near Washington, D.C. is "an American soldier known but to God." During public ceremonies the wreaths placed on the tomb in Paris honor all French heroes.

Napoleon's remains were carried beneath the Arch in 1840, and Victor Hugo was given the same funeral honor in 1885. The Etoile and the Arch have taken part in great episodes in French history, but those that occurred on certain days in 1918 and 1945 find no equals. Then the First and Second World Wars ended, and the armies marched in victory parades. Each war left terrible scars on the French nation. The scars, the courage, and the mortal cost of liberation are all engraved into the history of the Etoile.

The splendid plaza called the Place de l'Etoile, the Place of the Star, is often described as a giant wheel with twelve spokes, for twelve avenues spread out from its deep circle. At its center stands the Arch of Triumph, fully worthy of the superb setting. The Etoile has more importance than any other single area in Paris and is a masterpiece of design. Its plan was drawn by Baron Haussmann (1809-1891) whose genius as a builder left its lasting imprint on Paris.

The Champs-Elysées is a connecting stem between these foremost sections of the city, the Etoile and the Place de la Concorde. The stem forms part of a marvelous vista, nearly two miles long, reaching from the Arch of

Triumph southeastward to the Louvre Palace. In front of the Louvre's main entrance it is possible to look through the Carrousel Arch across the Tuileries Gardens, past the Obelisk in the Place de la Concorde, and up the entire length of the Champs-Elysées to the Arch of Triumph at the Etoile.

When people speak of the Louvre, they usually mean the world-renowned art museum in Paris, but this occupies only a part of the massive buildings that form the Louvre Palace, the largest royal dwelling ever built. All the kings of France made some use of the Louvre as a residence, from 1204, when King Philip Augustus built it as a for-

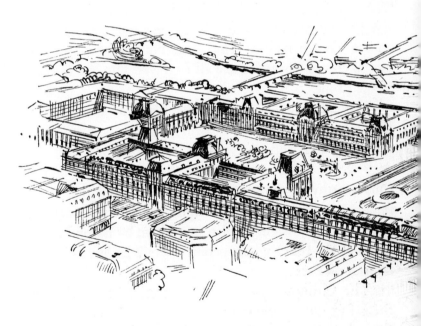

The buildings of the Louvre Palace; the Cour C
the Tuileries on the right

tress, until 1876. During their reigns most of these rulers improved and enlarged sections of their estate, spreading its walls until they enclosed forty-five acres. The Louvre contains hundreds of rooms and galleries, and miles of corridors. One is bound to wonder whether all of them have ever been explored.

The sixteenth-century king, Francis I, is remembered in French history as a patron of the arts. He bought many fine works and encouraged artistic talent all over Europe. After his time the royal collections increased rapidly. Louis XIV owned thousands of paintings. Napoleon I made the Louvre a national museum, to belong to the

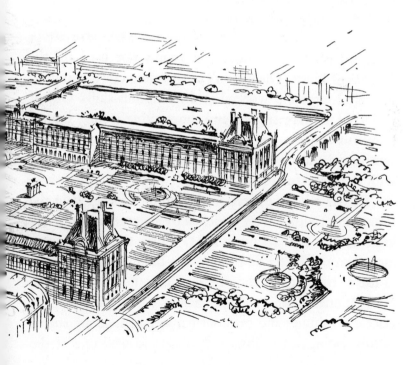

art-loving French people and provide a permanent home for the invaluable bequests of their monarchs.

The most historic part of the palace surrounds the Square Court (Cour Carrée) and extends along the Seine banks to the Carrousel Bridge. The museum occupies this long palace wing that borders the river. The parallel wing is a recent addition completed late in the nineteenth century. From the great court it stretches west along the rue de Rivoli, one of the most famous streets of Paris. The Place du Carrousel curves handsomely before the Louvre's central buildings and between the long wings, or arms, that reach toward the Tuileries Garden. Napoleon marked this plaza with the small but lovely Carrousel Arch, in further honor of his victories.

There was a time before Napoleon when workshops were set up in the Louvre, in rooms not used by the families of kings. The nation's outstanding craftsmen lived in these rooms and worked at their various skills. Out of these old Louvre studios and shops came a long line of beautiful objects for the royal masters, from jeweled snuffboxes and clocks to oil portraits and chandeliers, all with the graceful French touch.

The state book collections begun by Charles V in the fourteenth century were enriched by succeeding kings and kept in the Louvre until 1721. Then the books were moved to the Hôtel de Nevers, the building that remains in use as the core of the present Bibliothèque Nationale, the National Library. Thousands of the rarest and most priceless volumes and manuscripts in existence are stored in this distinguished library. It houses as well one of the largest general book collections in the world, but it is not a public library in the usual sense. Only scholars and advanced students are granted its full privileges.

From the last years of Louis XIV until the French Revolution, the eighteenth century brought changes of the greatest consequence to Paris. The last years of this eventful century saw two men create ties of affection between France and the United States which have never been forgotten. One of these was the wise and witty elder statesman, Benjamin Franklin, American Minister to France during a period when his young nation, struggling for its existence, needed friends. The French loved and respected Franklin. He died in 1790, shortly after his return home. In the meantime a youthful French nobleman had become an American idol and close companion of George Washington. He was, of course, the Marquis de Lafayette, who in 1777 joined the colonies' fight for their liberty. His own country soon would be fighting the French Revolution, which began in Paris in 1792, and was the bloodiest chapter in the city's long history. Napoleon Bonaparte gained power finally in 1799 and restored peace and order, before setting out to conquer the rest of Europe. The Napoleonic era ended in disaster in 1814.

After the downfall of Napoleon, and a period of changes, the Second Empire under Louis Napoleon (Napoleon III) brought a golden age of achievement to Paris, between 1850 and 1870. He and Georges Eugène Haussmann, more than any other men, are responsible for the features familiar to the world today as the face of Paris. Baron Haussmann was an important civic official, empowered by the full backing of Louis Napoleon for his tremendous tasks. The bold, imaginative works of Haussmann meet the eyes at every turn.

This far-sighted city planner was devoted to wide asphalt streets. By great fortune, generations of Paris builders were consistent in their taste for regularity. The avenues were designed to run long, wide, and free. Their clean lines allowed generously for open squares, and preserved the clear, uncluttered views. Formal plantings of trees and shrubbery were considered essential to the classic ideal in the city's design, and contributed greatly to its elegance. Haussmann opened the long vistas of streets and saw to their good drainage and good lighting. By 1865 twenty thousand gas street lamps illuminated Paris, and justly entitled her to be called "the City of Light." Haussmann designed the Etoile and Place de l'Opéra, established railway stations, and modernized the central market of Paris, Les Halles. He extended the network of boulevards to carry the city's increasing traffic.

Baron Haussmann also built the system of public parks that ring the city, and revealed the picturesque squares. Paris draws charm from these small "green islands of light and air." The lesser known squares, bordered by old houses, as well as the large and famous squares and public gardens are defended against change.

Place des Vosges, tucked away in a maze of rundown streets, preserves its flavor and original character. Henry IV built it in 1605, to give the crowded neighborhood a sunny space, and to ornament the city with houses of good design. It still makes a peaceful oasis, found by going

Place des Vosges

east on the rue de Rivoli, past the Town Hall. Another enclosure that seems related in atmosphere to the Place des Vosges is the Place Dauphine, on the Ile de la Cité. Its lines of old houses and trees are set in a V-shape, with a park in the middle. Place Dauphine frames a view of Henry IV's statue on the Pont Neuf, which pleases the eyes of many photographers.

Many squares and gardens are rooted in history. The Palais Royal is an example, meaning not the Royal Palace but the pleasant space it helps to enclose. Shops and houses line three sides of this garden, and the one-time palace of Cardinal Richelieu stands on the fourth, headquarters now for the Council of State, and housing also the national

*King Henry IV,
on his horse, still rides
on the Pont Neuf*

theatre. This quiet retreat from the city's noise, just north
of the Louvre, is cherished by writers and other artists.

The stately lines of the Tuileries Garden (Jardin des
Tuileries) connect the Place de la Concorde and the
Louvre grounds. The palace that stood in this park was
a favorite home of the rulers of France until the Revolution. It was from this house that the unhappy royal pair,
Louis XVI and Marie Antoinette, left to face the guillo-
tine. When fire destroyed the Tuileries Palace nearly a
hundred years later, it cleared the much-praised view from
the Louvre to the Arch of Triumph. The garden's *allées*
of clipped trees, sculptures, and ornamental ponds retain

the formality of the eighteenth century. Two statues of winged horses flank its entrance to the Place de la Concorde. Along the southern end of the Tuileries, fishermen sit relaxed with their poles on the shady banks of the Seine.

One of the statues at the entrance to the Tuileries

While Louis Napoleon and Baron Haussmann were modernizing and improving Paris, the city took the lead in several fields, particularly in fine arts. Paris literary circles were never more brilliant, with the fresh novels and poetry of Musset, Zola, Hugo, Balzac, Flaubert, Baudelaire, and Renan in the forefront. As to music, the opera and concert halls were acclaiming Berlioz, Offenbach, Bizet, and two composers from Italy, Cherubini and Rossini. Painting shared the favors of the era under its outstanding masters, Delacroix, Daumier, Manet, Corot, Courbet. The work in Paris of Louis Pasteur brought significant advances in medicine.

The French touch in cooking and home decorating was felt around the world. In women's fashions Paris assumed full command. Style-conscious women everywhere had long admired the smartly attired Parisiennes and had been happy to procure lengths of their lustrous fabrics, as well as their ideas on what should be done with them. The French fashion sense proved to be one of the state's most valuable assets, and developed a business empire of powerful scope. Lovely French-made clothes were henceforth ardently desired by women of means in every land.

The Franco-Prussian War in 1870 and 1871 brought these good times to a harsh end. Food supplies to Paris were cut off and the people came close to starvation. They ate whatever they could find, even devouring animals in their zoo. These bitter days finally passed, but their sorrow is remembered.

France again was a battleground in the two world wars

of the twentieth century. Fighting planes did, however, avoid the skies over Paris, and spared treasures of beauty that could never have been replaced.

For two thousand years history has been molding this capital of the French. The ancient spires rise above a valley that men in countless battles have fought to save. These men in every century have cared deeply for their homes and their freedom. Whether they bore arms as free men in the wars of France, or as enforced soldiers of a despot, they defended Paris as the jewel of their land. No Frenchmen were braver than the Underground fighters, the *maquis*, of World War II. Many of them died, but those who survived the German Occupation helped to liberate their city, in the glorious summer of 1944.

All dark shadows of the past seem invisible in the Place de l'Opéra today. It is called the crossroads of Europe because of the traffic that rolls over it from all directions.

This busiest center in Paris ranks next in importance to the Etoile and Place de la Concorde. Cars, buses, trucks, motor scooters, and bicycles clamor endlessly in and out of, around and about the Place de l'Opéra. Facing this open square stands the round-topped, ornate Opera House of Paris, L'Opéra.

Since it was completed in 1875, this theatre, which is one of the largest in use anywhere, has maintained its noted richness. The interior, in white marble with crimson velvet hangings and gold furnishings, provides a brilliant setting for the opera and ballet seasons. Triple-tiered boxes overlook the great stage. On gala occasions, members of the

Outside of Paris Opera House

Garde Républicaine, French guardsmen of highest renown, line the foyer's Grand Staircase. They stand like resplendent statues in their dress uniforms of red tunics, white trousers, and gold helmets with horsetails. Clusters of round lamps on the tall candelabra illuminate the whole spectacular scene.

Offices, theatres, stores, restaurants, banks, and shops of every kind surround the Place de l'Opéra. The streets that adjoin and fringe the square bear names that are always linked with high fashion in clothes. Place Vendôme, rue de la Paix, rue Royale, rue St.-Honoré are extremely well known to women who come from afar to buy the best. Some of the costliest dresses in the world may be purchased on the rue de la Paix, and everything expensive from sables to objects of art on the Faubourg St.-Honoré. A few leading Paris designers decide what will be fashionable in clothes next season. Their exclusive headquarters

The Grand Staircase in the foyer of the Opera House

Place de l'Opera, with Opera House in background

now mingle with some once historic residences. The Marquis de Lafayette lived at number 211 on the rue St.-Honoré, and Queen Marie Antoinette visited him there to congratulate him, when he returned home a hero after the American Revolution.

Place Vendôme can be seen from the Opera House by looking along the rue de la Paix. Here is the heart of the fashion kingdom. Its shops display the most lavish jewelry, furs, wearing apparel, and perfumes. The great banks and houses of finance are located in this square,

Place Vendôme with Vendôme column

Church of the Madeleine

named for the Duke of Vendôme, whose palace stood here. The composer Frédéric Chopin died in 1849 in the house at number 12. Place Vendôme's unmistakable features are its octagonal shape and the Vendôme Column, which is a monument to Napoleon, in its center.

Not far from Place de l'Opéra and Place Vendôme the beautiful Church de la Madeleine, like a Greek temple, with its classic pillars, faces the Place de la Concorde. The choicest array of fresh flowers in Paris brightens the side of this church. Here the central flower market's outdoor stands are enjoyed in all weather by the flower-loving

Parisians. Roses, violets, carnations, lilies are massed on pavements and benches under umbrellas and awnings. Flowers from the south of France are shipped daily into the capital, where they are always plentiful, and priced as cheaply as vegetables and other market necessities.

From La Madeleine to the Place de la Concorde is a short walk on the rue Royale, and a left turn at its corner joins the rue de Rivoli. Irresistible little shops line this lively street under its famous arcades and arches. Old buildings that overhang and shelter the sidewalks form the arcades. They make the rue de Rivoli a glowing stream of light at night, when a lamp hangs in every archway, down the long line to the Place des Pyramides.

Farther east along the rue de Rivoli, beyond the arcades, the Louvre wing, and Les Halles (the city market), a prominent plaza extends to the Seine and broadly borders it. This is the Place de l'Hôtel de Ville, which surrounds the town hall of Paris, otherwise known as the Hôtel de Ville. In this fine building the municipal government has its home. News pictures make the balcony familiar, as the place where distinguished visitors to Paris appear publicly. The First Republic was proclaimed at the Hôtel de Ville in 1870. After the Second World War, General Charles de Gaulle stood on its steps to announce the liberation of Paris, and, in a solemn moment in 1958, the birth of the Fifth Republic.

The Place de l'Hôtel de Ville lies near the heart of Paris, separated from Notre Dame only by a narrow channel of the river. Every Fourteenth of July crowds throng

Hôtel de Ville

The domes of Sacré Coeur, overlooking Montmartre

the square, as they do the Place de la Concorde, to celebrate Bastille Day. The people of Paris turn out in their gayest mood, and several orchestras around the square play for their dancing.

The famous hill of the Right Bank is Montmartre, called "*la Butte*" by Parisians, which means the Hill. Montmartre, the highest elevation in Paris, rises in the north. The immense white-domed church that crowns the top of Montmartre is Sacré-Coeur, one of the city's landmarks. It is visible from many parts of Paris, the dome shining softly through the mist, looking at times as if it floated in air. This is a modern church, finished in 1912, with the distinctive design of a huge central dome surrounded by smaller domes.

Those who climb the long stairway to Sacré-Coeur, or ride the funicular railway, may stand on the church terrace and gaze far over the city. A different Paris meets the viewer from the rear of the church, an industrial Paris of smokestacks belonging to the manufacturing suburbs.

Montmartre is the old "bohemia" of Paris. Most of the city's art life was centered there until the time of the First World War. The Place Pigalle, rue Lepic, rue Cortot, and other local byways were made notorious by the modern masters of painting, Renoir, Gauguin, Degas, Van Gogh, Toulouse-Lautrec, Picasso, Utrillo, and others. By 1920 the narrow streets climbing around *la Butte* were being deserted by artists and writers of major talent. They went to live in Montparnasse, an equally famous hill across the Seine, on the Left Bank, leaving Montmartre to the tourists.

Since then, restaurants and nightclubs have replaced many of the old studios in Montmartre, and the small streets and alleys are alive at night with sightseers looking for entertainment. On warm days, however, artists still paint outdoors in Place du Tertre, while people passing by look over their shoulders to see their work.

The new prophets of art around 1900 gave Montmartre its fame. They have left many valuable paintings and drawings describing the scenes they knew: the quaint squares, their hard-used studios, the smoky little cabarets, and especially the men and women who then lived the bohemian life of Paris.

If all parts of the north side of the city, this diverse

Artist and onlookers in the Place du Tertre

and wonderful Right Bank, were explored, their story might never end. But no explorer expects to finish the story of old and new, rich and poor, gay and careworn Paris.

Artists painted the scenes they knew

THE LEFT BANK

The most varied region of Paris and usually the liveliest is the Left Bank. It spreads south of the Seine, and contains enough famous places, history, and ideas to fill many books. Its quays, boulevards, and public monuments, its ancient churches, and above all its colleges and art colony supply local color of endless fascination. If its particular atmosphere has been brewed by ages of history, the Left Bank nevertheless is known for setting a modern pace.

The Luxembourg Palace and Gardens, St.-Germain des Près, the Latin Quarter, Montparnasse, Boulevard St.-Michel are just a few of its points of interest. The very words "Left Bank" suggest freedom, and young people excited about causes. But on the Left Bank there is also devotion to art and to learning. The places where students gather are special centers of activities. Artists' cafés and galleries also are plentiful. The book trades are located in this section of Paris, with publishers, printers, binders, and bookstores occupying many streets. Some of the finest book bindings obtainable anywhere in the world are tooled in the cramped, dark quarters of small local business houses that have preserved their talent exactly as they inherited it.

As for books, the stalls along the Seine that sell second-hand copies are the typical, time-honored trademark of the Left Bank. They have lined the quays on both sides of the river for centuries. *Le bon roi Henri*, the good King Henry, permitted them to open for outdoor business in 1603, on the barely completed Pont Neuf. They spread to the quay-bordered riverbanks, and have flourished best on the Left Bank's Quai Voltaire. Books overflow from shelves and boxes that rest by old habit along the shaded parapets of this street of literary tradition.

The booksellers on the quays tend their stalls in hot and cold weather, on fair days and foul. They are a hardy breed of men, but they give up when it rains, for water ruins their books. The long green-painted boxes then are closed. These outdoor merchants, called *bouquinistes*, are expert judges of book values. Customers often like to hunt among the used copies and publishers' bargain lots, in the hope of discovering a rare volume overlooked by the seller, that can be bought for less than its value. They are seldom successful.

From early times in Paris, abbeys and schools were established on the Left Bank. The venerable abbey church of St.-Germain des Près stands on the Boulevard St.-Germain, still embodying the region's early history. Some of the building stones in its bell tower were set into the church foundation in the year 1020. These are the oldest

Book stalls on the Left Bank

St.-Germain des Près and café on Left Bank

material still in use in all Paris, and make the building, and it only, more ancient than Notre Dame.

In its youth this Left Bank abbey was wealthy and powerful. Warrior monks fought off the invaders here. Settlements on the Ile de la Cité extended their growth toward St.-Germain to come under its protection. Between the church and the river lies a section of old, old streets which seem to have changed but little in the modern centuries.

The Boulevard St.-Germain, winding through the

upper Left Bank, is a street of great reputation. The church neighborhood at its eastern end is crowded with shops which make Paris the leading antique center of the world. Hundreds of other places offer for sale everything new in art and in literature. Small hotels and rooming houses (*pensions*) are numerous, each dominated by its *concierge*, or caretaker, who is a formidable personality in Paris. The *concierge* may be a man or a woman, but

A typical concierge

in any case is an authority on all matters concerning his paying guests.

The spacious western end of the Boulevard St.-Germain retains its aristocratic style. Many of its exclusive residences have passed into public use as embassies or legations. After the seventeenth century, noblemen were attracted to the Left Bank by the grandeur of Les Invalides. They found nicely wooded land available and established their family seats. Their mansions were responsible for making the section east of Les Invalides, the Faubourg St.-Germain, known as "the noble Faubourg."

Latin students congregating on the Left Bank in the Middle Ages, when colleges were forming, gave the name "Latin Quarter" to the student area. In those days education specialized in religious doctrine and Latin was the chief subject taught. Ever since then the Latin Quarter has been the domain of college students. The schools of higher learning center around the Sorbonne, ancient college of the University of Paris, now in the seventh century of its existence. Its modern courses in the arts and sciences bring scholars to Paris from all over the world.

There is no livelier street in the city than the Boulevard St.-Michel. The students named it "Boul Mich" and have made it their special territory. They crowd around the tables of their favorite Boul Mich restaurants and keep lights burning till late at night. Thousands of students enable the Left Bank to preserve its reputation for energetic spirits and active ideas.

Montparnasse is the Left Bank's hilltop. Artists and writers, as mentioned earlier, came from Montmartre to

Sorbonne

live on its slopes, and through the years younger artists
and writers, as well as art schools and galleries, have fol-
lowed them. Ingres, Manet, Picasso, Modigliani, Utrillo,
Braque are some of the modern artists who have given the
area its vitality. Many well-known men and women have
lived in Montparnasse, some of them obscurely for a while,
or as exiles from their native lands. The old revolutionaries
in art and literature, and the spectacularly talented, have
in a measure been replaced by a less exciting middle class.
But art students and other hopeful young people do still

flock to this part of Paris, to work and study near masters of their crafts. Their discussions produce a stimulating atmosphere in the restaurants where they meet.

Parisians are interested in their artists and deeply proud of their city's regard for all creative work. Objects of art surround the citizens of Paris all their lives, and influence their tastes from the beginning. This luxury capital of the world has been called the paupers' paradise, because there is enough fine art in public places for everybody to enjoy every day. The rich architecture, the symmetry of streets with their trees and green *allées,* the fountains and abundant statuary remind Parisians to observe what is beautiful, wherever they come across it.

The homeless of other lands have often found refuge in Paris. The unusually gifted who live there have bestowed their talents upon her, giving their best whether native born or adopted citizens. The free spirit of the city has been their inspiration. They may live on very little money, as many in Paris do. Often garrets are cold in winter. But in the small cafés these people are welcome to sit for hours, free to talk and to dream of new work, and to share their problems with congenial companions. A cup of coffee or glass of wine is enough to order. Some of the loneliness and isolation of big cities are broken down in Paris by the brotherhood of the humble cafés.

In some poorer Left Bank sections the age of the houses is astonishing. Stone masonry was an honored craft in the Middle Ages, and Frenchmen possessed such knowledge of their materials that what they built has lasted. On new construction jobs builders dig down to the remains

3 rue Volta, the oldest residence in Paris

of old walls and old pavements, and use them as modern foundations. The oldest residence known in Paris remains solid in structure. It is number 3 in the rue Volta, and it has been lived in continually since it rose on that spot, incredibly long ago, in the year 1240.

Off the Boulevard St.-Michel medieval-looking streets are crooked and too narrow for sunlight. The aged houses are badly kept. A woman comes from the market at the corner with vegetables in a string shopping bag, and the ever-present long, unwrapped loaf of bread. A priest passing by stops to talk to the children who play in the street. Their school building in the next block looks like its surroundings, old and in need of repairs.

Not far away is a pleasant place for these boys and girls of a shabby Left Bank neighborhood. In rue Boutebrie a library called L'Heure Joyeuse, which means The Joyous Hour, has been welcoming young Parisians for

A typical narrow, crooked street

many years and offering them books to enjoy. Most libraries in Paris are for university students and scholarly adults, but this one is similar to the kind children know in the United States. In fact it was established with American help, after the First World War. The Joyous Hour shows by its appearance that it means what its name says. Its inviting open shelves hold wonderful books of all kinds. Boys and girls come to read what they like, and the li-

off the Boulevard Saint-Michel

Baron Georges Eugène Haussmann

brarians help them find it. They look at picture books and listen to stories, and sometimes get material for their school lessons, just as American children do.

Paris children have a favorite park on the Left Bank, the always delightful Luxembourg Gardens. There they have good times watching Punch and Judy shows, sailing their painted boats on the lake, and riding the carrousel.

The Luxembourg Palace, where the widow of Henry IV once lived, provides a stately background for the gardens. It stands in a direct line with the Louvre Palace, which is due north of the Luxembourg. No Paris gardens are more beautiful than the flower-bordered paths and lawns of the Luxembourg (Jardin du Luxembourg), or more loved by all Parisians. Some say that Roman coins can still be dug up among the tulip bulbs, for Roman legions were quartered here when Paris was Lutetia.

Luxembourg Palace and Gardens

PLEASURES AND TREASURES

Everybody discovers personal treasures in Paris, for no city offers them more liberally. Many are free to the public, and easy to find. Those that give the most pleasure seem to be part of the timelessness of the city, the same today as yesterday. Passing events do not change the real treasures of Paris. When one begins to choose what is appealing, great treasures and small pleasures are always mixed up together. Take this mixture: the Grand Gallery in the Louvre Museum, a bowl of onion soup early in the morning at Les Halles, and the Rond Point at night, lit up by its glowing fountains. Which is the favorite? A few typical choices do prove this much: Paris treasures have variety, and pleasures are scattered all around.

Paris is a world art center because of the Louvre Museum. The Louvre houses one of the greatest collections of treasures in all fields of painting, sculpture, ceramics, tapestries, covering all periods from ancient to modern. Only the British Museum in London and the Metropolitan Museum in New York are ranked beside it in importance. No work of art is acceptable to the Louvre until ten years after the artist's death. Thus, all political and personal influences are forgotten, leaving only the quality of the workmanship to be judged.

The galleries contain an unimaginable wealth of paintings, with Italian and Dutch masters in special strength. Leonardo da Vinci's *Mona Lisa* is the Louvre's most notable attraction. This portrait of a lady faintly smiling holds a magnetic appeal never equaled on canvas. Mona Lisa's secret expression draws thousands of admirers in never-ending lines. So many people come into the Louvre especially to see this picture that the museum guards, without waiting to be asked where it hangs, sometimes point at once in the direction of the thickest crowds. Francis I bought the *Mona Lisa*, also called *La Jaconda* or *La Gioconda*, directly from the artist. It has therefore been owned by France all the four and a half centuries of its existence.

The antique sculpture collection on the Louvre's ground floor possesses another supreme prize, the *Venus de Milo*. This marble figure of the Greek goddess stands in complete majesty, apart from other Grecian sculptures. Pictures in books have made this Venus as familiar as the Statue of Liberty, but she is far more beautiful than they reveal. The statue was carved in the second century B.C., and found on the island of Melos in 1820.

At the head of a staircase, in thrilling view, stands another world-famous sculpture, the Winged Victory (or Nike of Samothrace). This priceless relic of the fourth century was excavated from the Greek island of Samothrace in 1863. Great sculptures by Michelangelo, Dona-

A king's room in the Louvre Museum

tello, and Cellini are displayed in the Louvre, and other uncountable attractions lure the visitor down every corridor. The way to enjoy these great collections is to go to the Louvre again and again, seeing just a little each time.

The Louvre Palace and Notre Dame Cathedral are the most illustrious monuments in Paris. The Museum's riches in all branches of art include the additional glories of its architecture and history. The rooms that show how three kings (Louis XIV, XV, and XVI) lived, attract popular interest. These have been preserved with their elegant fittings and many private possessions collected during these fabulous monarchies.

Food for the mind and spirit is never wanting in Paris, but food for the palate is one of the city's crowning delights. All of it comes from the sprawling general market of Paris, Les Halles Centrales, which is as Parisian in tradition as the Louvre or the Eiffel Tower. The novelist Emile Zola called it "the belly of Paris." For over eight hundred years Les Halles has clung to an area east of the Louvre, bounded by the Boulevard de Sébastopol, and reaching on the south closer and closer to the Seine. It was rebuilt by Baron Haussmann, under Napoleon III, between 1854 and 1866. Since then the market sheds have had to push outward in all directions. With the coming of automobiles the narrow streets around Les Halles became bottlenecks, choked with trucks and crates of produce and lines of congested traffic. The procession of vegetable trucks begins about ten o'clock every evening, streaming into the city from all sides. They roll heavily along the quays and through the Place de l'Opéra, piled high with onions, cabbages, tomatoes, lettuce; others with eggs, cheeses, game, fish. The oversized meat trucks barely scrape through side streets originally meant for horse-drawn wagons.

Because of the traffic problems around Les Halles there is talk of dividing it and moving sections to various new locations in the outer parts of Paris. The move will be gradual, if it takes place, and many years will pass before the old market district disappears and the last burlap bags are swept away.

In daytime the buildings and sheds are drab and the streets around them empty and shabby. But through the night Les Halles is in its glory with the colors, shapes, and smells of the wonderful foods of Paris. Its busiest hours are between two and four in the morning, while most of the city sleeps. Trucks unload crates of carrots and baskets of fruit onto the sidewalks. Florists arrange their stalls of flowers, and farmers their strawberries and cauliflowers, with equal care. Butchers in blood-soaked aprons carry meat from the trucks.

At dawn the homely sheds are full of beautiful merchandise, carefully displayed, with all of a kind in one place: pale mushrooms in even mounds, eels from Brittany, pink crabs, shrimps, cockles; trout from the Pyrenees, beans and scallions from the truck farms outside Paris, flowers and grapes from the whole countryside. Much of all this is sold to the little neighborhood markets, and some even to individuals who are up that early, or out that late. But hotels and restaurants buy the choicest varieties. Soon in a thousand huge kitchens chefs wearing tall white hats

A restaurant in Les Halles

will give orders to their helpers, and these lovely foods will be served in the superb French style.

Meanwhile the various restaurants in Les Halles fill with customers, some in evening clothes next to truckmen in overalls, and the familiar aroma of onion soup floats over the sheds. Onion soup is the specialty at market eating places, which have odd names such as The Quiet Old Man, The Pig's Feet, The Smoking Dog. One way to conclude an evening of entertainment in Paris is at Les Halles, eating onion soup, and afterward wandering among the flower stalls buying bouquets at bargain prices. Then,

Fountain of the Innocents

in a square at the northeast end of the market district, the visitor must see the Fountain of the Innocents, a gem of sculpture by Jean Goujon.

Two of France's most precious products are created in Paris, Sèvres porcelain and Gobelin tapestries. Sèvres, on the Seine in the city's western outskirts, is the home of the world-famous potteries established there in 1753 by Louis XV. A visitor enters the main building through gardens, and finds himself in what was formerly a palace but is now the Sèvres Museum. Behind it are factory buildings and kilns four stories high where the porcelain is fired. The place to linger is in the exhibition hall, where the display of fine china shows what is meant by Sèvres art. The tableware, clocks, vases, and other objects are absolutely exquisite in texture and colors. There is free range in design, even modern pieces being accepted, but the new ideas have to meet Sèvres standards of quality. The entire production represents ceramic perfection. Every worker is an artist, sometimes descended from generations of Sèvres artists. The non-profit plant is owned by the government, and any pottery manufacturer in France can obtain advice from these experts.

Another remarkable institution, and French craftsmanship of a different order, may be enjoyed by following the Avenue des Gobelins on the Left Bank to the Gobelin Museum and factory. This is the home of the finest tapestries in the world, and like Sèvres, is government-owned. The Gobelin family were dyers and weavers in Rheims before they moved to Paris in the mid-fifteenth century.

A Gobelin tapestry on the wall and Sèvres porcelain on the table

So painstaking was their work, one weaver would produce no more than three or four yards of tapestry in a year. During the Gobelin period of great glory in the eighteenth century, the kings appointed special artists just to draw the weavers' patterns, which then were created in fabric with countless colors and shadings. Gobelin tapestries hang in the great buildings of France, and occasionally in a foreign capital when the French government has presented one of the pieces as a gift. Very rarely is a tapestry sold. On certain days visitors may attend exhibitions in the Gobelin Museum and see into the workshops, where weavers and power looms still perform with their intricate skill.

The French people love animals, and pets have an important place in their family life. Small breeds of dogs are the most popular, such as Pekinese, Scotties, poodles, and particularly dachshunds. All kinds of animals and birds that children want to own are found in the pet shops on the rue de Rivoli. And there is also a bird market, open only on Sundays, where individuals display birds they want to sell. When favorite pets die, there is a beautiful and melancholy place for some of them, on a quiet island in the Seine.

This graveyard is Le Cimetière des Chiens (The Dog Cemetery), in a northwestern suburb of Paris. There are graves of dog champions, war dogs, some plain mongrels, dogs that belonged to famous people, and even a motion picture star, the original Rin Tin Tin.

A St. Bernard of fifty years ago named Barry has the

largest monument in the cemetery, near the entrance. The lines engraved under his statue tell that he saved forty persons before he was killed by the forty-first, a smuggler whom the border patrol pursued in an Alpine pass. Barry had found the fellow lying wounded in the snow, and stretched his huge body over him, as St. Bernards are trained to do, to keep him from freezing. The smuggler revived, and killed the dog in order to avoid capture.

Le Cimetière des Chiens

The cemetery, originally intended for dogs only, now holds about forty thousand animals. Most of them are dogs and cats, but two horses, a circus lion, monkeys, rabbits, several birds, and a hen also have places.

Hundreds of sad-faced people walk along the ceme-

tery's shaded gravel paths on Sundays, reading the names on the small tombstones and remembering their own lost pets. School children come in groups on other days. At one monument they have patted the lifelike faces of a pair of stone dogs until their noses shine. Families bring flowers to plant on the graves, and sit silently under the trees. Many have placed framed pictures of their dogs or cats on the tombstones. One very touching stone is shaped like a doghouse, standing open-doored and empty. Another tombstone dated 1900, among the earliest, has this pathetic message: "To my little dog. I am all alone now and no longer have anything to live for." A memorial to a dog called Clown says, "You who so amused us, now you make us weep."

A walk on the Avenue des Champs-Elysées is gayer, and indeed one of the very special pleasures. When spring comes to Paris, fleur-de-lis like our blue iris blooms in flowerbeds on the lawns, and up and down the avenue white blossoms burst on the chestnut trees. Families stroll together and children play on grassy stretches beside the Champs-Elysées. Some of them wait in a group to see a Punch and Judy show. The same puppet characters of Punch and his wife Judy, with their dog, Toby, have been telling the same well-known stories for centuries. This is the French children's *Guignol.* The little puppet theatre is ready and the curtain rises on the comedy. Punch whacks away with his stick, Judy raps back, and the children laugh and clap. The balloon man comes along with a

bounding pack of colors and shapes, and children with
sous in their pockets swarm around him trying to decide
which one to buy.

Two statues of rearing horses, held by their tamers, are
dramatic guardians of the entrance to the Champs-Elysées
from the Place de la Concorde. These are the Horses of
Marly (Les Chevaux de Marly), by Coustou, mounted on
high pedestals. Now the sound of live horses stirs a flurry
of excitement along the street, and a mounted detachment
of the Garde Républicaine appears in all its regalia, flash-
ing red, blue, and gold. People stop whatever they are
doing to watch these guardsmen, who have a great appeal
to the popular fancy. They are an honor troop, called out
for escort duties or to serve at state ceremonies and occasions calling for pomp. Their white-trousered uniforms and
plumed helmets, their glittering breastplates and swords,
and brightly polished boots make these soldiers the pride
of Paris. They never make a more thrilling spectacle than
when they ride on the Champs-Elysées.

For a century street lighting has been part of the tradition of beauty in the capital. At velvety dusk the three-
globed street lamps strung along important boulevards
glow soft green-gold through the haze. After dark the
fountains are lit, and floodlights on ancient churches and
on stone-wrought monuments renew their life, and revive
the creamy tones of their youth. Shining fountains illuminate the Rond Point, and the Obelisk is a fresh new shaft
of pink, with the Arch radiant in the distance. Then the
Champs-Elysées is in sparkling mood, and the Paris of

"gaiety and light" is in her element, unspoiled by time and smoke.

The practical yet sensitive Parisians love their city with intense devotion. Their moods respond to the varied atmosphere of Paris, and they are moved by her past as well as by her present fortunes. Violence, glory, genius, and sacrifice have brought many experiences, and have left their mark.

A misty day on an old street brings an air of melan-

The Garde Républicaine parading down the Champs Elysées to

choly to the houses, and the very stones look weary. On brighter days the silvery Paris sky looks down on a smiling city. Whatever the weather, Paris has grace and harmony.

Among the celebrated cities of the world, Paris is the great lady. She wears many faces. One of them is old and proud, remembering the luster in her past. Another looks eternally young, the Paris of chestnut trees, springtime, and romance. Something is here for everyone who comes to know this gay, wise, enchanting Queen of the Continent.

the Place de la Concorde, which is guarded by the Horses of Marly

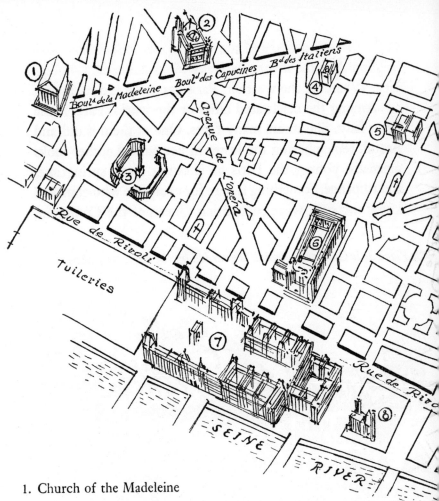

1. Church of the Madeleine

2. Opera House

3. Place Vendôme

4. Opéra Comique

5. Bourse

6. Royal Palace

7. Louvre

8. St. Germain des Prés

9. Tour St. Jacques

10. Hôtel de Ville

11. Place des Vosges

A walk on the rue de Rivoli on the Right Bank from
the Church of the Madeleine to Place des Vosges

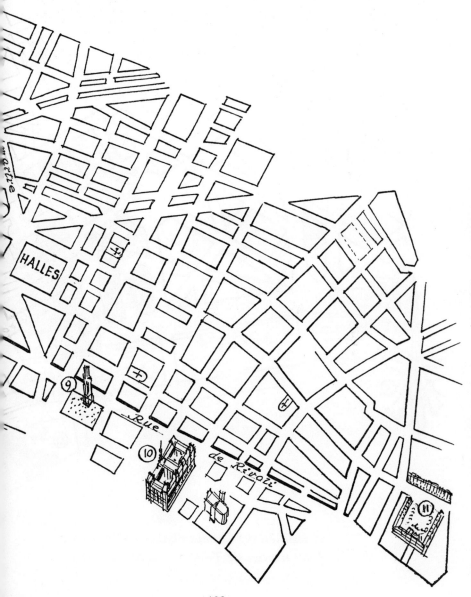

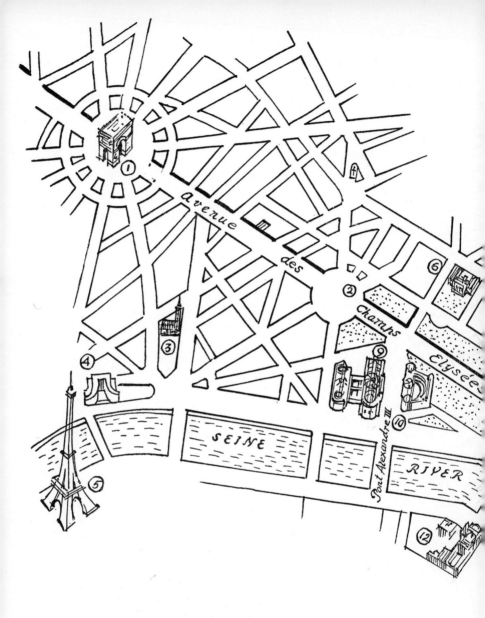

A walk on the Champs Elysées (Right Bank)
from the Arc de Triomphe to the Louvre Palace

1. Etoile and the Arch of Triumph
2. Rond Point
3. American Church
4. Chaillot Palace (Museum of Man)
5. Eiffel Tower
6. Elysée Palace

7. American Embassy
8. Church of the Madeleine
9. Grand Palace
10. Petit Palace
11. Place de la Concorde
12. Bourbon Palace
13. Louvre Palace
14. Tuileries Garden

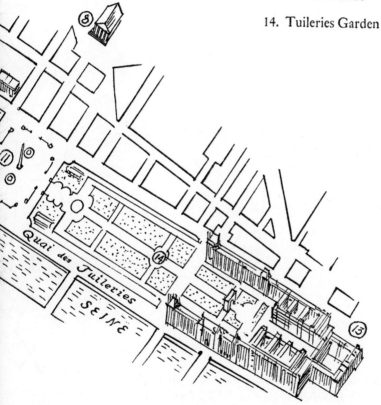

A walk on the Boulevard Saint Germain (Left Bank)
from the Bourbon Palace to Ile St. Louis

1. Bourbon Palace
2. Palace of the Legion of Honor
3. Gare d'Orsay
4. Pentemont Temple
5. Medical College
6. St. Germain des Prés
7. St. Sulpice
8. Luxembourg Palace
9. Odéon
10. Palace of Justice
11. Police Headquarters
12. St. Severin
13. Cluny Museum
14. Sorbonne
15. College of France
16. Notre Dame Cathedral
17. Louvre
18. Institute of France

A walk in Montmartre (Left Bank)

1. Sacré Coeur

2. Montmartre Garden

3. Moulin Rouge

4. Place Pigalle

5. Circus

6. Humour Theatre

7. Tabarin

8. Guignol Theatre

9. Pigalle Theatre

10. Folies Bérgère

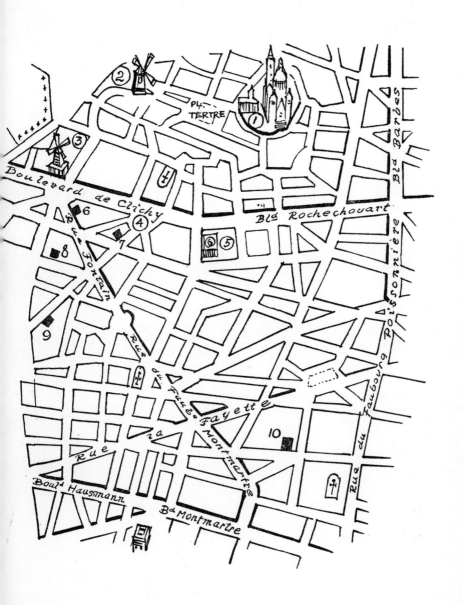

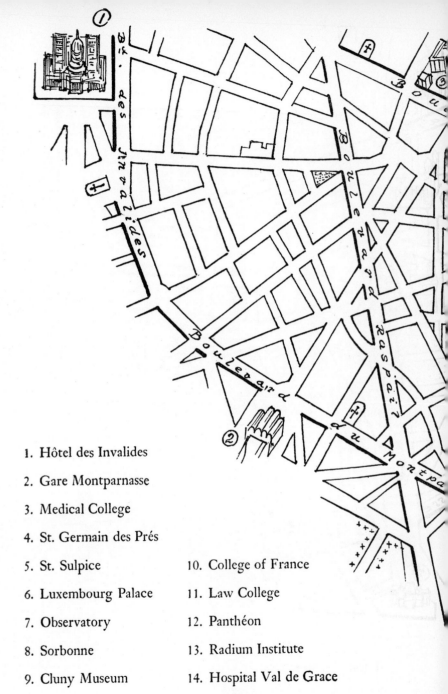

1. Hôtel des Invalides

2. Gare Montparnasse

3. Medical College

4. St. Germain des Prés

5. St. Sulpice

6. Luxembourg Palace

7. Observatory

8. Sorbonne

9. Cluny Museum

10. College of France

11. Law College

12. Panthéon

13. Radium Institute

14. Hospital Val de Grace

A walk in Montparnasse (*Left Bank*)

117

PRONUNCIATION GUIDE

Listed below are all the French words that appear in the text. They are listed by chapter, in the order of their first appearance. No word is repeated.

French and English are, of course, two quite different languages, and there is no way to give you exact pronunciations. There are some sounds used in French that are not used in English. The only way really to learn a foreign language is to hear it spoken.

Therefore, this guide offers only an approximation of the way these words sound—close enough, we hope, so that if you want to ask a *gendarme* how to get to the Louvre, or want to order *croissants* for breakfast, you will be understood.

This sign (') is used after the accented syllable. When it is possible to give an English syllable to indicate pronunciation, that has been done. Otherwise, the following system has been used.

		English	French
a	as in	bat	Paris
â	as in	bar	Lazâre
e	as the a in	villa	le
ĕ or è	as in	when	for the ein in Seine or the e in Sèvres
é or es	as the ay in	play (except that you cut it off very short)	Sacré
ō	as in	no (but cut off short)	Notre Dame
o	as in	rob	brioche
u	as in	brunette	charcuterie
ou	as in	root	Boulogne

	English	*French*
ŏ, eu, or ŭ as the nio in	onion	{ Boulŏgne
		{ Monsieur
gn as the u in	fun	Boulogne

French words containing the letter n are the hardest to approximate, because n in French has a nasal sound that we do not use. If you pinch your nostrils and say "Sa" with the a pronounced as in "bat," you will have a rough idea of the way the French word "Saint" is pronounced, or the "in" in the word "Vincennes." If you do the same, but pronounce the a like "on", you will have an approximation of the "ants" in "croissants." When this "n" is used, it appears in parentheses (n).

CHAPTER I

Paris	pa-ree'
Cherbourg	share'-boor
Le Havre	le hâv'-re
Gare Saint-Lazare	gar sa(n) la-zâr'
Orly	or-lee'
Le Bourget	le boor-zhay'
Sacré-Coeur	sa-kray kur
Champs-Elysées	shah(n) zay-lee-zay
la Seine	la sĕn
Île de la Cité	eel de la see-tay'
Notre Dame	nō-tre dam'
croissants	krwah-sah(n)'
brioche	bree'-ōsh
charcuterie	shar-koo-tree'
tabac	ta-back'
rue	ru
Montmartre	mō(n)-mar'-tre
lycée	lee-say'
arrondissement	a-rō(n)-dees-mah(n)'
gendarme	zha(n)-darm'
centime	sah(n)-teem'

Bois de Boulogne	bwa de boo-lŏgn'
Vincennes	va(n)-sĕn'
Jardin des Plantes	zhar-da(n)' day plah(n)t
Parc Monceau	park mō(n)-sō'
Montsouri	mo(n) soo-ree'
Saint Cloud	sa(n) kloo
Sèvres	sè-vre
mont	mō(n)
Valerian	va-lay-ree-yah(n)'
Boulogne-Billancourt	boo-lŏgn bee-yan-koor'
Saclay	sa-klay'
Versailles	vair-sigh'
Fontainebleau	fō(n)-ta(n)-blo'
monsieur	meu-syeu'
madame	ma-dam'
soufflé	soo-flay'

CHAPTER II

Ile Saint-Louis	eel sa(n) loo-wee'
Lutèce	lu-tèss'
Domrémy	dō(n)m-ray-mee'
Place des Pyramides	plass day pee-ra-meed'
bateaux mouche	ba-tō moosh
Solférino	sol-fay-ree-nō'
Pont Royal	pō(n) rwa-yal'
quai	kay
Vert Galant	vair ga-lah(n)'
Pont Neuf	po(n) neuf
Pont des Arts	po(n) day-zar'
Grand Palais	grah(n) pa-lay'
Petit Palais	ptee pa-lay'
Quai d'Orsay	kay dor-say'
l'Hôtel des Invalides	lō-tĕll daze-a(n)-va-leed'
chasseur	shah-suhr'
Zouave	zwahv
la tour Eiffel	la toor ĕf-fĕll'
Palais de Chaillot	pa-lay de shy-yo'

Musée de l'Homme	mu-zay de lum
Pont de Grenelle	pō(n) de gre-nĕll'
Sainte-Chapelle	sa(n) sha-pĕll'

CHAPTER III

Place de la Concorde	plass de la kō(n)-kord'
Etoile	ay-twahl'
Louvre	loo'-vre
l'Opéra	loh pay-rah'
Vêndome	von-dome'
Grands Boulevards	grah(n) bool-var'
la Madeleine	la mad-lĕn'
Bastille	bas-tee'
Porte Saint-Denis	port sa(n)-de-nee'
Saint Martin	sa(n) mar-ta(n)'
Rond Point	rō(n) pwa(n)'
Marseille	mar-say'
Lyon	lee-yō(n)'
Strasbourg	strahz-boor'
Lille	leel
Rouen	roo-ah(n)'
Brest	brest
Nantes	nant
Bordeaux	bor-do'
Elysée	ay-lee-zay'
Arc de Triomphe	ark de tree-ō(n)mf'
Tuileries	twee-le-ree'
Cour Carrée	koor ka-ray'
rue de Rivoli	ru de riv-o-lee'
l'Hôtel de Nevers	lō-tĕll de ne-vair'
Bibliothèque Nationale	beeb-lee-ō-tĕk' na-see-ō-nal'
Les Halles Centrale	lay hal sĕn-tral'
Place des Vosges	plass day vozh
Place Dauphine	plass do-feen'
Palais Royal	pa-lay rwa-yal'
allée	al-lay'
maquis	ma-kee'

Garde Républicaine	gard ray-poob-lee-kĕn'
rue de la Paix	ru de la pay
Faubourg Saint-Honoré	foh-boor sa(n) tō(n)-ō-ray'
l'Hôtel de Ville	lō-tĕll de veel
butte	but
Pigalle	pee-gal'
Lepic	le-peek'
Cortot	kor-to'

CHAPTER IV

Luxembourg	lux-ah(n)m-boor'
Saint-Germain des Prés	sa(n) zher-ma(n) day pray'
Montparnasse	mō(n) par-nass'
Saint Michel	sa(n) mee-shĕll'
bouquinistes	boo-kee-neest'
pension	pah(n)-see-ō(n)'
concierge	kō(n)-see-yairzh'
Sorbonne	sor-bŭn'
Boutebrie	but-bree'
l'Heure Joyeuse	lur jwa-yeuz'

CHAPTER V

Gobelin	gō-bla(n)'
le Cimetière des Chiens	le seem-tyair day she-ah(n)'
fleur-de-lis	fleur-de-lee
guignol	geen-yole'
sou	soo
Les Chevaux de Marly	lay she-vo' de mar-lee'

INDEX

Cimetière des Chiens, Le, 101-104
Cleopatra's Needle, *see* Obelisk of Luxor
Colbert, Jean-Baptiste, 48
colleges, *see* schools
concierge, 83-84
Concorde, Place de la, 57, 64, 67, 72, 73, 105; location of, 46; description of, 49-54; obelisk in center of, 50, 58; original name of, 51; buildings on, 54; celebrations on, 54
cooking, 24-25, 66
Corot, Jean B. C., 66
Cortot, rue, 76
Council of State, 63
Cour Carrée, 60
Courbet, Gustave, 66
Coustou, Guillaume, 105

Daumier, Honoré, 66
Dauphine, Place, 63
da Vinci, Leonardo, 93
de Gaulle, Gen. Charles, 73
Degas, Edgar, 76
Delacroix, Ferdinand, 66
Denis, Saint, 28
districts, municipal, 20
Dog Cemetery, 101-104
Donatello, 93-94

Eiffel, A. G., 39
Eiffel Tower, 12, 13, 37-39
Elysée Palace, 54
Eternal Light, 54
Etoile, 49, 54, 57, 58, 62, 67; location of, 46; and French history, 57
Etoile, Place de l', 57

fashions, 66, 68-69, 71-72
Fifth Republic, 73
First Republic, 73
fishermen, 28, 32, 65
Flaubert, Gustave, 66

flower market, 44, 72-73, 96, 98
Foch Avenue, 21
Fontainebleau, 23
foods, 16, 25, 66, 95, 96, 98
Fountain of the Innocents, 99
fountains, 13, 86; of Bois de Boulogne, 21; of Versailles, 23; on Place de la Concorde, 50; at Rond Point, 92; on Champs-Elysées, 105
Fourteenth of July, 54, 73, 76
France, capital of, 11, 22, 25; provinces of, 11; shopkeepers of, 15; industries of, 22; cooking of, 24; early name of, 28; war of, with England, 30; home of President of, 54; and the United States, 61
Francis I, art collection of, 59; and *Mona Lisa*, 93
Franco-Prussian War, 49, 66
Franklin, Benjamin, 17, 61
French Revolution, 48, 51-52, 61, 64

Gabriel, Jacques, 51
Garde Républicaine, 68, 105
Garden of Plants, 22
gardens, public, 20-22, 58, 60, 63, 64, 79, 90; of Versailles, 22-23; of Grands and Petit Palais, 35; on Quai d'Orsay, 36
Gare St.-Lazare, 11
gargoyles, 42
Gauguin, Paul, 76
Gaul, 28
gendarmes, see police
Geneviève, Sainte, 28
Gioconda, La, 93
Gobelin factory, 99, 101
Goujon, Jean, 99
government, city, 20, 73; federal, 25
Grand Palais, 35
Grands Boulevards, 46, 48

sidewalks, 18, 28, 33
Solferino Bridge, 31
Sorbonne, 84
Square Court, *see* Cour Carrée
squares, 13, 20, 99; design of, 48, 62, 63; *see also individual names of*
statues, 30, 33, 39-41, 49, 63, 85; on walls of Notre Dame, 42; at entrance to Tuileries, 65; of horses, 65, 105; *see also* sculpture *and individual names of*
Strasbourg, statue for, 49
streets, 13, 15, 60, 62, 86; famous, 13, names of, 16-17; number of, 16; following Seine, 31-32, 36; in Montmartre, 76; on Left Bank, 82-83, 84, 87-88; around Les Halles, 95; *see also* boulevards, squares, *and individual names of*
students, 11, 16; on Left Bank, 79, 84, 85-86; and libraries, 88-90
suburbs, 11, 22-23, 76, 101
subway, 17-18

Tabac signs, 16
Tertre, Place du, 77
theatres, 64, 68; *see also* Opera House
tobacco, sale of, 16
Toulouse-Lautrec, Henri de, 76
Tour Eiffel, *see* Eiffel Tower
Town Hall, *see* Ville, Hôtel de
trades, *see* industry *and* people, work of
traffic, confusion of, 12, 13, 14, 17, 18; over bridges, 28, 33-34, 35; on Champs Elysées, 49; Haussmann and, 62; on Place de l'Opéra, 67; at Les Halles, 95-96
trees, 12, 19, 31, 49, 62, 64, 86, 104

Triomphe, Arc de, *see under* Arc de Triomphe
Tuileries Gardens, 58, 60, 64-65
Tuileries Palace, 64

United Nations, 39
United States, and France, 61
United States Embassy, 54
University of Paris, 48, 84
Unknown Soldier, of France, 54, 57; of America, 57
Utrillo, Maurice, 76, 85

Valerian, Mont, 22
Van Gogh, Vincent, 76
Vendôme Column, 72
Vendôme, Duke of, 72
Vendôme, Place, location of, 46; and fashion, 68, 71; features of, 72
Venus de Milo, 93
Versailles, 22-23
Vert Galant, Square du, 32
Ville, Hôtel de, 63, 73
Vincennes, Bois de, 21
Volta, rue, 87
Voltaire, 16
Voltaire, Quai, 80
Vosges, Place des, 62-63

Washington, George, 17, 61
weather, 22, 37
Wilson, Woodrow, 17
Winged Victory, 93
World War I, 66-67; and Etoile, 57; changes in Montmartre after, 76
World War II, 66-67; and Place de la Concorde, 54; and Etoile, 57; Hôtel de Ville and, 73

Zola, Emile, 17, 66, 95
zoo, 21, 66
Zouave, as water-gauge, 37

128